EARLY

A Piccolo Factbook

Contents

EARLY MAN

By Anne Millard

Editor: Jacqui Bailey

Series Design: David Jefferis

A Piccolo Factbook

Discovering Early Man

In 1650, after making a long and careful study of the Old Testament, Bishop Ussher announced that God had created the world in October, 4004 years before the birth of Christ. And that, as far as most people were concerned, was that. It was therefore upsetting when a few scholars produced the remains of men and of primitive tools, which they insisted were millions of years old.

At the time, most people refused to believe the scholars. But although it is hard to imagine, we now know that our ancestors were living in caves and hunting their food more than 50,000 years ago.

Darwin and Evolution

Above: Charles Darwin (1809-1882). On his voyage, Darwin visited the Galapagos Islands. He noticed how creatures like the finch (below) differed slightly on each island. He realized this was due to the different environments in which they lived. In 1859, he published his ideas in a book called *On the Origin of Species*.

By the 19th century, many scholars had realized that the Earth was much older than Ussher had ever dreamed. This meant that there were now millions of years to be accounted for, during which many kinds of animals could have flourished and died. There were even some people who said that modern animals had evolved from strange, very ancient creatures.

Natural Selection

One of these people was Charles Darwin. He had observed many animals on his voyage round the world in

1831. He claimed that when their surroundings changed, the plants and animals had to change too or they died. The animal that could run faster, reach further, grip tighter or think better would live longer and pass its advantages on to more offspring. By this 'natural selection' process those that adapted best survived. The new skill would grow with each generation until a new kind of creature developed, or evolved, from the old.

So modern plants, animals and people must have evolved out of earlier forms.

Buried Clues

If Darwin was right and modern plants and animals evolved from those that lived long ago, then a study of

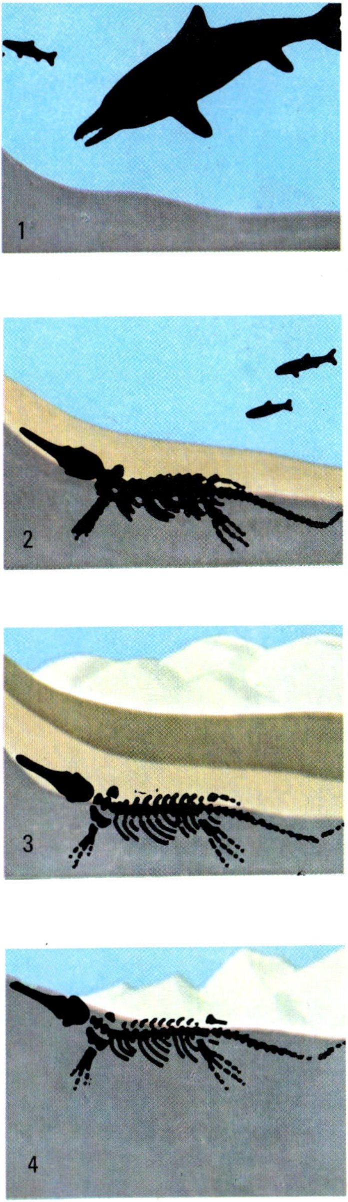

Millions of years ago a sea creature died and sank to the sea bed (1). Its body was quickly covered with sand and mud. Its flesh decayed, but its bones remained and minerals from the water and mud entered tiny holes or pores in the bones, making them like stones (2). Over hundreds of years, movements in the Earth lifted the sea bed out of the water (3). Wind and rain wore away the surface rock until the fossil skeleton was exposed (4).

fossils could prove it.

Fossils are the hardened, rock-like remains of plants or animals that were alive millions of years ago. They are formed when a living thing is buried by sand or mud. Millions of years later, the fossil can tell us many things about itself and what the Earth was like when it was alive.

By studying such ancient remains, Darwin's ideas about the slow change of one type of animal into another were proved to be right.

Evolution at Work

About 55 million years ago, there was a little animal called *Eohippus*, the ancestor of modern horses. It was about 30 centimetres tall and had four toes on the front feet and three on the back. It lived in forests and its teeth show that it ate leaves. As time passed, a new, larger breed appeared with three toes on each foot. The great forests gradually changed into grasslands, but horses survived because they could adapt to eating grass.

Necks became larger. So did the middle toes on each foot, until horses walked just on one toe on each foot. This gave them the speed they needed to escape enemies.

Eohippus (dawn horse), 55-40 million years ago

Mesohippus, 40-25 million years ago

Merychippus, 25-10 million years ago

Pliohippus, the ancestor of modern horses, asses and zebras

Four stages in the evolution of the horse from about 55 million years ago to some 5 million years ago.

Digging Up History

If you examine a single stone tool, you can work out how it was made. Perhaps you can also judge the skill of the maker.

If you are next given a complete set of tools from one place, you will know if the ancient owners used a wide variety of tools for different jobs. You can work out what the jobs were and so learn a good deal about how they lived.

Objects in the Ground

You will learn even more if you find the tools in place in the ground. The stone they are made from will tell you if the tools were made locally or if they came from elsewhere, which suggests travel or trade.

Suppose you find two different sets of tools in the same general area. Does that mean there were two different tribes living there? Or was one tribe doing different jobs in different parts of the same area? If you decide it was one tribe, this will suggest how they lived and how well organized they were. It is by studying buried objects in this way that an archaeologist pieces together the history of life in earlier times.

Archaeologists at work. Great care is taken so as not to disturb or damage the finds.

Missing Links

When you walk around a big museum, you will probably be impressed by the large number of objects displayed. It is hard to understand why there are so many gaps in our knowledge. But just think of the Earth's age and how much we have lost.

We have seen (page 9) that very special conditions are needed to make a fossil. Think of the billions of animals and people who did *not* die under just the right circumstances. Then it seems incredible that we have learned as much as we have about the history of life on Earth. Think, too, of all the destruction that has taken place over the centuries – tomb robbers, mining, wars, earthquakes and so on. So the archaeologist's work is vital.

How Old?

It is an archaeologist's job to recover information about the past by excavating (digging up) ancient remains.

Much can be learned of people's daily life and beliefs from the objects they bury with the dead for use in the 'next world'.

But there is a serious danger with this. When you dig up a site, you destroy it, so you must find everything and record every detail. As we have seen, it is not just objects that are important. It is also where they came from, and when.

People did not invent ways of writing until about 3300 BC. Dating objects made before then is a very hard task. You can study classes of objects and work out which are the early forms and which the later ones, but that does not give you an actual date. If a site has been lived on for a long time, layers of debris build up and the oldest things are at the bottom. But this still does not tell you when they were made.

It is only with the help of modern scientific methods that archaeologists today are able to discover the information they need.

Dating Techniques

There are a number of ways of discovering something's age. Carbon 14 dating (right) gives us approximate dates up to about 50,000 years ago. A method called *thermo-luminescence* can be used on objects that have been burnt, such as pottery or stones heated by camp fires.

RADIO CARBON
(CARBON 14)
DATING

Radiocarbon from the air is absorbed as carbon dioxide by plants. People and other animals eat plants and the radio-carbon enters their bodies too. After death, no more Carbon 14, as it is called, is absorbed. Instead, it is given off at a steady rate. By measuring how much is left we can find out the age of a piece of wood, charcoal, bone or shell.

By cutting a trench down through a site you can learn its history from the layers. The trench below reveals remains of early hunters and farmers at the bottom. Then come other farmers who dug post holes to build a wooden stockade. This was later burnt by invaders who put up buildings of stone and dug a rubbish pit down into previous layers. Archeologists spend much time studying layers like these.

Dating by tree rings (right) is useful for more recent objects, when samples of tree ring patterns are more readily available.

Archaeology and Science

Scientific techniques help archaeologists in other ways too. By examining soil from an archaeological dig under a microscope you can find the pollen grains of long dead plants and trees. These can

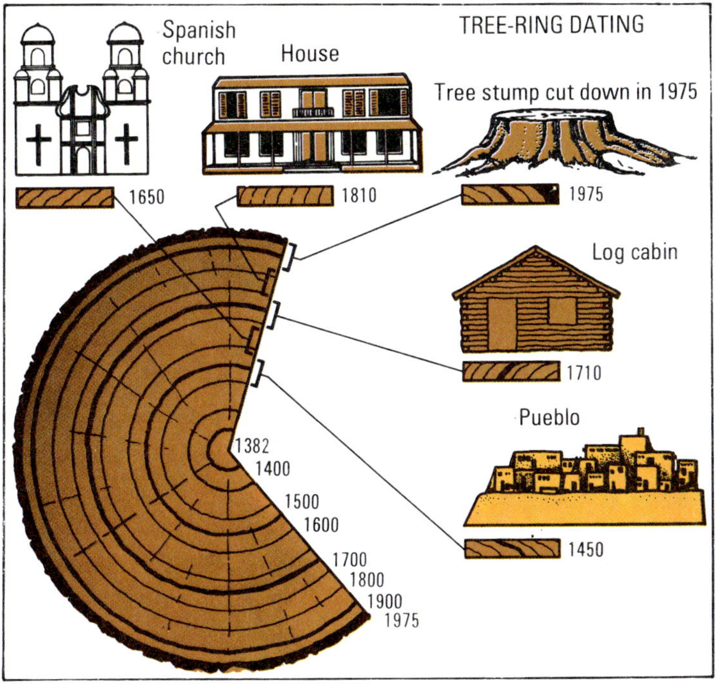

tell us what used to grow in the area. This, in turn, will show what the climate used to be like and so what food was available for gathering.

Examining a specially cut, thin slice of a piece of pottery or stone with a microscope will enable you to see exactly what it is made up of. Stone and clay vary from place to place, so you can work out where it came from. If the object was discovered a long way from where it was made, this tells you something about ancient trade routes.

Every year a tree lives it grows an extra ring round its trunk. In a good season it will be a wide ring, in a bad one it will be narrow. Trees in the same area have similar patterns of rings. Starting with a modern tree you look for older wood with ring patterns that overlap with those already known. If you can find enough examples with matching rings you can work back through the past. The tree above goes back 600 years, but, in the south western USA, sites as early as AD 11 have been dated.

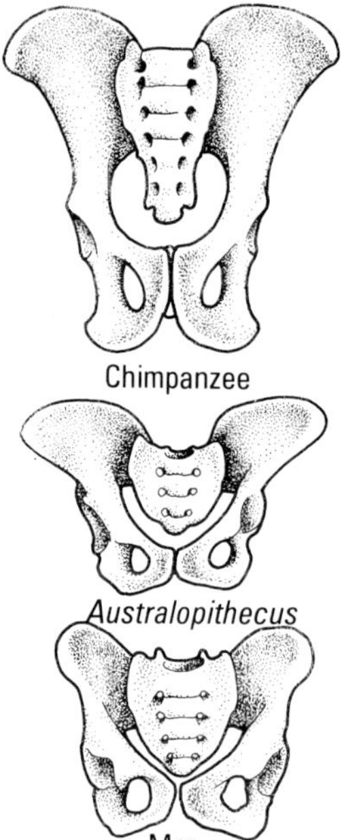

Walking upright alters the pelvis (hip bones). By examining the pelvis, it is possible to tell if a creature walked like a man or an ape.

What Makes Us Human?

Gorillas and chimpanzees are our closest living relatives. Not only do we look alike, we even share some of the same diseases. Yet there are crucial differences.

Ways of Walking
Humans stride along on two legs, holding themselves upright. Our ape cousins have a rolling gait and balance themselves on their knuckles most of the time, so they have long arms and powerful shoulders.

Walking upright has freed our hands for continual use. By using them for a variety of tasks we have changed the way our thumbs work and have become more skilful.

Human teeth are smaller and are arranged in a slightly

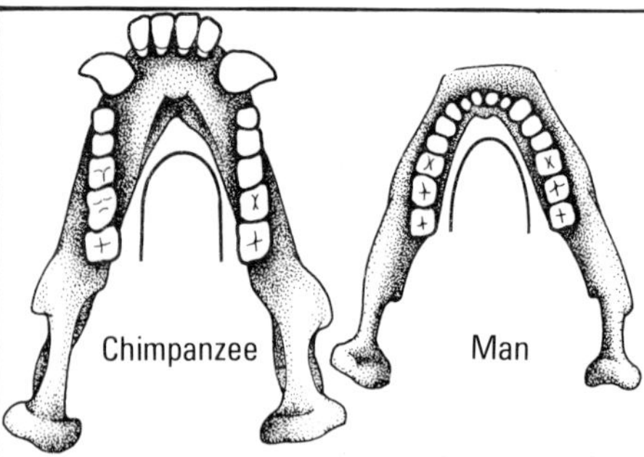

An animal's teeth show what kind of food it eats by their shape, size and arrangement. As our ancestors changed their diet their teeth became less ape-like. So teeth are vital clues.

different pattern. This means our facial muscles are smaller too and we do not have ridges over our brows, or large jaws.

A Bigger Brain

Most important of all is the large and very complex human brain. Compared to other animals, we have lost some of our sharpness of sight, smell and hearing. But in their place we have gained the power of reason.

With our powers of reason we can work out the answer to a problem, store the solution away in our memories and then, by using our other special skill of speech, pass the stored information on to others.

Since these are the special features that set us apart from our ape cousins, we must begin the search for our remote ancestors by looking for ape-like creatures, which show one or more of these human features.

But before doing so we must take a step backward, to the rise of the mammals.

Apes are clever and have enough control over their hands to do quite complicated things like opening locks. But only humans have thumbs that move so freely that we can perform the most delicate tasks and grip firmly to lift heavy objects.

The Successful Mammals

Some 200 million years ago, reptiles ruled the Earth. There were a great many different kinds of reptiles at that time and some of them were real giants. You would not have thought that there was any need or room for any other kind of animals to evolve! Yet, in the rocks of that remote age, a few traces have been found of the fossil remains of some entirely new kind of creatures – the mammals.

The first mammals were small, insignificant beings. They needed to be if they were to escape the attentions of the great dinosaurs, some of whom were flesh-eaters. But the little newcomers had some interesting adaptations, which helped them to survive when the world's climate changed and the mighty dinosaurs, who could not adapt to the new conditions, died out.

With the reptiles gone, some mammals evolved into flesh-eaters like this jaguar. Others ate only plants.

Still others ate anything that was going! Though small, rats and mice can live almost anywhere.

The Adaptable Mammal

Reptiles are cold-blooded creatures. They take their body temperature from the air around them, so when it is cold they are sluggish. Mammals were different: they had warm blood. They had, as it were, built-in central heating, which enabled them to move around fast and freely, even at night when there was no sun to warm them. They had also evolved a new, effective covering for their bodies. Instead of scales like reptiles, mammals had fur, which helped to keep them warm.

Reptiles lay eggs, often leaving them to hatch out by themselves. A few mammals, like the platypus, lay eggs. Some other kinds (marsupials), such as kangaroos, keep their babies in pouches. Most mammals, however, are placental. This means the mothers keep their babies joined to them in their own bodies until they are well grown. When a baby mammal is born its mother feeds it on milk produced by her own body. Thus, from the very start, a baby mammal has a good chance of survival.

A Small Beginning

Among the early mammals were primates, the family to which man belongs. The first primates were small shrew-like creatures with beady eyes, long snouts and whiskers. They ate anything they could find, probably coming out at night when it was safe. That was about 65 million years ago.

It took about 5 million years for the Earth to change and the dinosaurs to die out, but then mammals came into their own and populated and soon took over the Earth.

The Tree Dwellers

One group of primates had taken to the trees and done very well. These prosimians were larger than their shrew-like forbears and they had evolved a good grip for climbing. Their noses were smaller and their eyes were now in the front of the face, so they had the better sight they needed. Life in moving branches is dangerous, so the brain also developed, to allow problems to be dealt with quicker.

But the prosimians were largely displaced by two branches of their own family who had adapted even more successfully to tree-living, the monkeys and the apes.

Left: This African bush-baby is one of the few prosimians alive today. The others are lemurs and tarsiers.

Below: This little meat-eating creature was one of the first primates. It was no bigger than a dinosaur's egg.

Out of the Trees

Compared to life on the open plains, trees offered monkeys and apes shelter from danger and a safe place to sleep. But some of the early apes, either seeking new sources of food or perhaps from curiosity, began spending more time on the ground.

These apes had always to be on the alert for danger but they could also take advantage of new opportunities. To cope with this demanding new environment better brains were needed.

One of these adventurous apes, who lived about 15 million years ago, has been given the name *Ramapithecus* and he was a very important discovery.

Unlike the other apes, the ancestors of the gibbons stayed in the trees. Nowadays, gibbons are so well adapted to this life they rarely venture on to the ground.

Left: Among the types of ape who did leave the trees, there may have been one who was to become our earliest form of ancestor.

'Rama's Ape'

What makes *Ramapithecus* so exciting are his teeth. They were not truly ape-like. There is just a hint of human appearance about these teeth, which may mean he is one of our oldest ancestors. We have only a very few of his remains, so we need to find more to see what his hands were like and if he had started to stand upright.

Ramapithecus was certainly a successful character. Traces of him have been found in India, Africa, China and Europe. After him there is a gap in our records, until about 5 million years ago when the first signs of a new ape-creature, *Australopithecus*, appear on the scene.

'Southern Ape'

Australopithecus was a most unusual ape. His remains, found in Africa, show he was only about 1.3 metres tall, but he stood upright on two feet. This would make him more visible to enemies, less agile to dodge and feint and less well balanced. On the other hand, he was a good lookout and his hands were free to carry food away to safety.

Man-Like Hominids

It was once thought that *Australopithecus* was a toolmaker and a direct ancestor of man. Now it seems neither theory is correct. Recent excavations have revealed the existence of other creatures, who lived at the same time as the Southern Apes, but are considered to be more man-like in appearance. They are grouped as 'hominids'.

One of these hominids was named *Homo habilis* (Handy Man) by his discoverer, indicating his belief that this was a man-like creature and a maker of tools.

Other experts do not accept the separate existence of Handy Man. They say some of the specimens found are *Australopithecus* and others belong to another, more advanced creature that we shall be discussing later (page 28).

There is also another creature, called simply 1470, because he has not yet been properly classified. He is certainly well on the way to being human. Clearly what is needed now is more excavation and new finds to help solve the problem.

Tool-Making and Meat-Eating

We must wait awhile for these problems to be sorted out, but one thing is clear. Living alongside the Southern Apes there were other, more human creatures of one or more kinds, who had made two spectacular advances – they had started making stone tools and they were building rough shelters out of rocks.

It seems likely that the Southern Apes, like apes today, lived mainly on plants and fruits, tasting meat only rarely and almost by chance. The hominids, like Handy Man and 1470, ate plants, roots and fruits and took eggs and baby birds when they could get them. But they had also taken to regular meat-eating. At first they probably just cleared up after a big cat had killed, but then they deliberately went after and killed slow-moving or sick animals and helpless young ones.

This reconstruction shows a group of ***Australopithecus*** **peering over the rocks on the far left, at a family of more advanced hominids who are building a windbreak of rocks.**

The First Shelters

Although the only traces of hominid constructions that have been found have been windbreaks made of rocks or animal hides, there must have been earlier experiments in building, which have disappeared without trace.

A group of apes will claim a territory round which they move gathering food. At night, wherever they happen to be, they make themselves beds from leaves and branches.

Our remote ancestors probably did the same. But some may also have bent branches together over themselves to make a roof. Yet others may have pulled off branches and driven them into the ground, so making shelters just where they wanted them.

The First Tools

In the wild, chimpanzees have been seen to break off a stick and trim it with care. They are making tools. They use these tools to poke into termite nests and bring out the insects, whose taste they seem to enjoy.

Our ancestors probably began their careers as tool-makers in a similar way. But they did not stop at one tool. On the open plains there must have been certain roots they especially enjoyed eating. Perhaps some genius worked out that it would be easier to dig for the roots with a stick, or bone from an old kill, than with his hands.

The first tools were very simple but also quite effective, like a sharp stick used to dig up roots for eating.

It is also easy to imagine that a primitive man might have used a stone to crack a nut or even open a shellfish. Any piece of rock would do for that. Then someone found out that by breaking a stone they would have a tool with a sharp cutting edge, which would be useful for a number of tasks.

Discovering Weapons

A chimpanzee faced with a leopard (stuffed and placed deliberately in its path, though of course it did not know that) has been seen to grab at a branch and wave it, clearly trying to drive off the enemy. Such meetings must have often happened in the remote past, but with live enemies.

Our hominid ancestors, unable to outrun a killer, grabbed up something to defend themselves. If the trick worked, it would be remembered and improved upon.

In this way early man acquired weapons. The same materials and objects that could be used for weapons – sticks, stones and bones – were also used as tools.

Mankind had taken a giant step forward in its development. But the hominids were soon to be surpassed.

Australopithecus

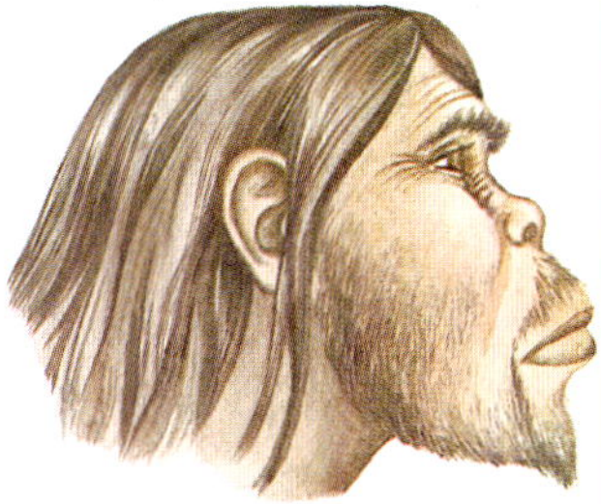

Homo habilis

Homo erectus

These reconstructions show how the different types of early men slowly became more human-looking.

Upright Man

About one million years ago *Homo erectus* (Upright Man) appeared. He had evolved from the hominids in less than a million years. The pace of progress had definitely speeded up.

Everyone agrees that Upright Man, with his larger brain, was well on the way to being human.

Upright Man's remains are found right across Asia and in Africa, and some of his more advanced descendants travelled into Europe.

Technical Progress

Upright Man was making better tools. He made hand axes by chipping flakes from either side of the stone. This gave a thinner and sharper cutting edge.

Upright Man and his descendants certainly needed better tools. Their remains show that they had taken to hunting big game. They had also learnt the use of fire!

The larger brain, improved hunting techniques and the discovery of fire all combined to produce another new and far-reaching development – the growth of the family group.

Below: The main stages and dates in the development of early man. The drawings show the changing shape of the skull and jaws and the more upright walking position.

THE ANCESTRY OF MAN

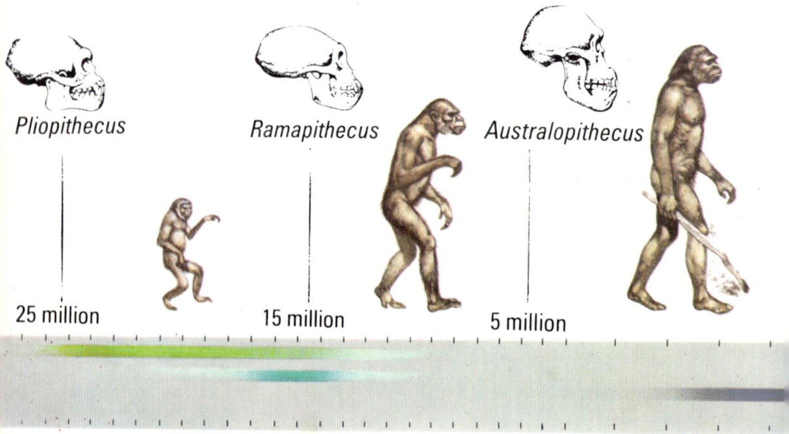

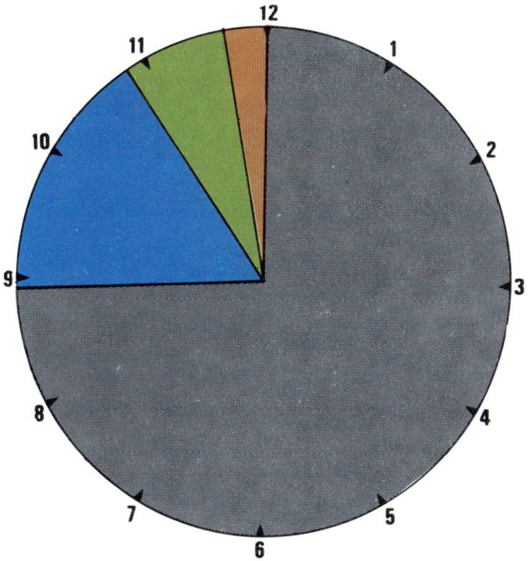

If the whole history of the Earth, some 4700 million years, was represented by one 24-hour day, then the animals who left fossils did not begin to appear until nearly 9 o'clock at night. The Age of Reptiles begins at nearly 11 p.m. Mammals appear just after 11.30 p.m., and man arrives in the very last minute before midnight.

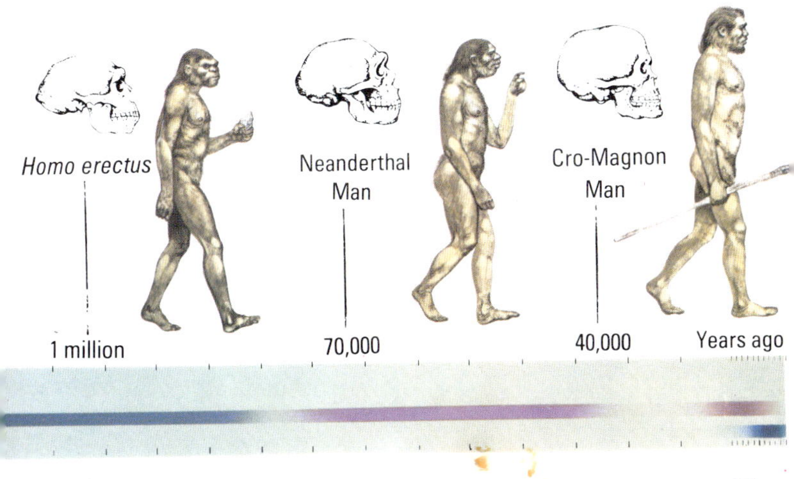

Family Man

When a baby monkey is born, its brain is already three-quarters the size of its parent's. Our ancestors had slowly evolved much bigger brains, but at birth they were comparatively small and it took many years for the brain to grow to full size. So human babies needed to be looked after for many more years than before. The need to protect their young led our ancestors to develop a new way of living.

The Home Base

Human mothers have no fur for their babies to cling to in the way monkeys do, nor can young children run fast enough to escape danger. In order to rear their babies successfully, human mothers began to need a safe place to stay in for long periods. For the first time, people began to look for more permanent shelters (above).

Monkeys and apes move as they feed. On the open plains our ancestors too roamed every day looking for food. Those who could not keep up soon fell victim to one of the many waiting killers. A twisted ankle or a stiff back was fatal.

When they began using home bases to protect their children, our ancestors also provided a safe place for the old and the sick. So more people survived and the numbers of humans grew.

The Human Family

In a troop of monkeys or apes like the baboons in the picture below, each one feeds itself. There is no idea of sharing food with other members of the troop. Man is the only primate that has learnt to do this. As women spent increasingly more time looking after their young, it became necessary for men to find food for their mates and their children.

The instinct that led men and women to co-operate in this way gradually developed to include feelings of affection within the family group, and a responsibility to the older members.

As the population of mankind increased, the co-operation between family groups began to spread outward to include other groups and eventually whole tribes.

Using Fire

Animals are afraid of fire and early man was no exception. But at some time a few individuals must have overcome this fear and snatched a burning stick from a natural fire that had started nearby (right).

Keeping Warm
Having lost most of their body hair, our ancestors had probably already begun wrapping animal skins around themselves for extra warmth. The use of fire meant they could now survive in much colder climates.

It was probably a long time before they learnt how to make their own fire. If his fire went out, early man would have had to steal a burning log from someone else's.

Learning to Cook
One day, probably by accident, someone may have dropped some meat in a fire. When they came to eat it, they found that they enjoyed the flavour of the cooked meat, so from then on cooking became the custom.

The desire to cook their kill would draw the hunters back to the home base, and encourage them to share the meat with their families.

Cooked meat is softer and easier to chew than raw meat, so over a period of time peoples' teeth, jaws and face muscles became smaller because they had less work to do. This made them look more like us.

Fire as a Weapon

People knew animals were afraid of fire. They must have seen otherwise dangerous enemies backing away from it. It was a short step to using fire for defence and then to using it for attack. People must have often wanted to shelter in caves during bad weather, only to find a fierce animal had got there first! With fire they could drive such animals out and take possession themselves. Fire became a powerful weapon.

Light

Once, like all other creatures that hunted by day, early man had gone to sleep when the Sun set. The possession of fire freed him from dependence on the Sun for light and it gave him leisure time. By the light of their camp fire a group of early people could sit, when the work of the day was done, and talk. They could plan future hunting expeditions and listen to the wisdom of the older people of the tribe.

Each group probably had one person to guard the fire and keep it alight.

Hunting

To hunt big game armed only with weapons of wood and stone takes great courage. There has to be a very good reason to risk many lives seeking such prey.

Although big game hunting was extremely dangerous for early man, it was very rewarding in terms of the amount of meat gained. The killing of small game is an individual effort. It only produces enough food for one or two people. But a few men who make a big kill will have enough meat not only for themselves, but for many others as well.

Because big game hunting required strength and was dangerous, it was the men who went out on hunting parties for their tribe. The women, who were already tied down to the base camp by the need to care for the children, turned their attention to gathering a variety of plant foods from the land around the camp.

In this way, men and women began to behave in increasingly different ways from each other.

Working Together

To be successful at big game hunting our ancestors had to learn to work together as a group. They had to study the ways of the game herds and work out plans of attack.

One effective method was to frighten their victims with noise and fire. The herd or animal could then be stampeded over a cliff or into a marsh and finished off with rocks or pointed sticks. The meat was then cut up and carried home to the tribe.

The Great Ice Age

About two million years ago the climate started slowly changing. It got steadily colder and colder. In the north, where the changes were most marked, the grasslands gave way to pine forests. Then, as the ice advanced still further, even the pine forests could not survive. Along the edge of the ice were treeless plains called tundra.

Map showing the extent of the great ice sheets.

Immense rivers of ice began to move across continents. We call these moving sheets of ice 'glaciers'. They pushed their way south, cutting out valleys and grinding down mountain tops as they went, until about one-third of the Earth's surface was covered by ice.

Four times the glaciers advanced and retreated across the northern half of the world. Today, you would have to go to the Arctic Circle to get an idea of what conditions were like then in Europe.

Some Ice Age glaciers would have dwarfed the skyscrapers of New York.

On the Move

It was the custom of the big game hunters to follow their food supply.

As the glaciers advanced, incredible amounts of water were frozen into ice caps. This meant that the level of the sea fell, exposing areas of land that had once been on the sea bed. Thus islands and continents that had been cut off from each other by water for millions of years were now joined by land bridges.

Britain was joined to the rest of Europe. Areas of the North Sea were dry land and the continents of Asia and America were linked by land in the north at what is now the Bering Straits. Naturally, once these land bridges had emerged, animals began to wander across them. The horse and the camel, for example, left America for Asia, while bison, bears and men went the other way. These animals settled in the continents they occupy today.

The map below shows the parts of the sea that became land in the Ice Age, and some of the creatures that crossed the land bridges.

Animal Adaptation

Those animals who needed warmth and could not adapt either died out or moved further south.

Those that remained became specially adapted to life on the tundra. Most famous of these are the mammoths, with their great curving tusks, and the woolly rhinos with their two horns.

These creatures died out at the end of the Ice Age, but other animals followed the ice and are still to be found in the Arctic. Among them were the reindeer, a favourite source of food for the ancient hunters.

Warm Interludes

There were warmer spells in between the movement of the glaciers. These are known as the interglacials. Then the trees and animals returned to the north, and woodland creatures like the beaver were plentiful.

As the wandering herds of animals crossed from one continent to another, small groups of people followed behind them.

Sometime between 40,000 and 25,000 years ago some of these groups crossed from Asia into America. These were the ancient ancestors of the American Indians.

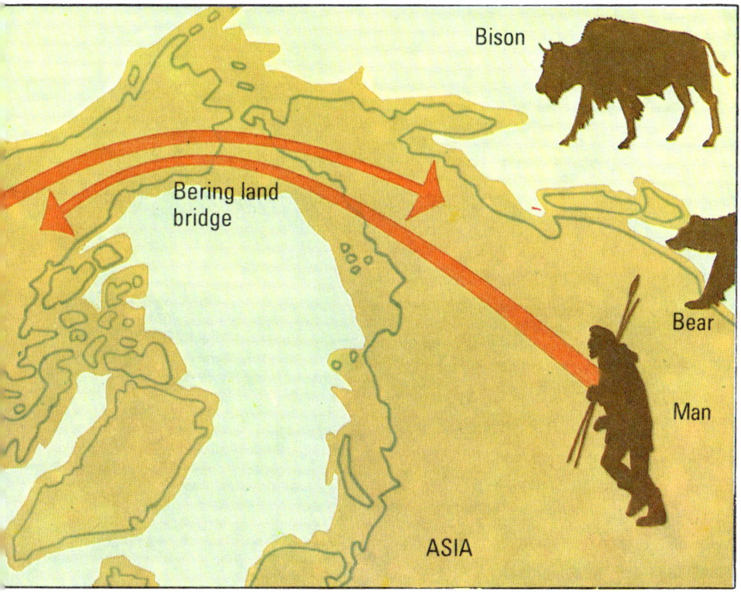

Neanderthal Man

With our usual lack of modesty, we call our branch of the family of man *Homo sapiens* (Wise Man). He is a descendant of Upright Man and he first appeared about 100,000 years ago.

One of the earliest known types of 'Wise Men' are called Neanderthals, after the place in Germany where their remains were first found. They lived in Europe some 70,000 years ago, during the last Ice Age.

Neanderthal Man was about 1.5 metres tall, with a strong, stocky body. His brain was larger than ours.

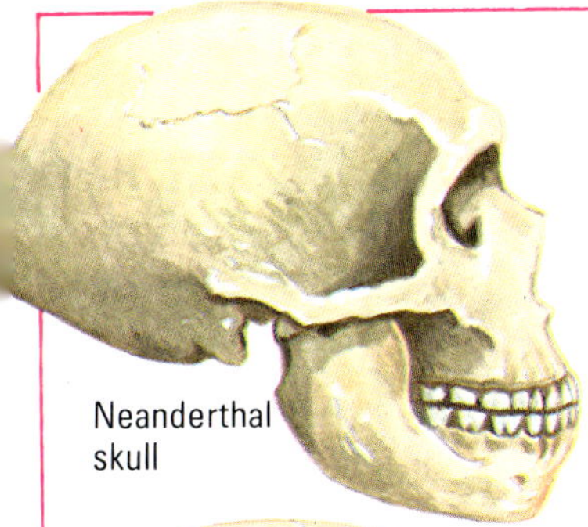

Neanderthal skull

Neanderthal Man

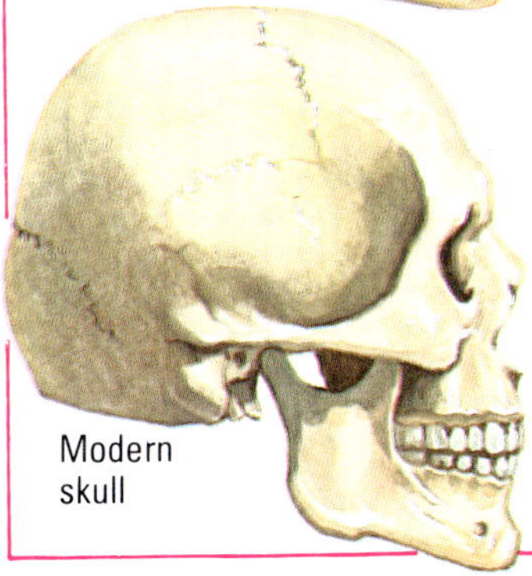

Modern skull

Compare the skull of modern man with that of Neanderthal Man. Our skulls have a rounder shape. We have higher foreheads and well-formed chins, but our teeth are smaller and our brows and jaws are not so heavy. Our skull shape appeared about 40,000 years ago.

Life in the Ice Age

We can only admire the way the Neanderthals survived the intense cold of the Ice Age winters in Europe.

Of course, fire was of vital importance. In places where wood was scarce, they probably burnt animal bones. Animal hides and furs were used for clothes. Also, the presence of foot bones of fur-bearing animals such as the fox, lynx, wolf and panther, around a prehistoric hearth suggests that fur bedding was used.

Food and Shelter

Caves, where they could be found, were obviously good shelters from the weather. But screens and tents, made of poles covered with skins and weighted down with stones or bones, were also essential for protection against the bitter wind and frost.

In winter, the snow must have often been too deep to go out hunting. Neanderthal Man must have fed on dried meat or meat frozen in the snow.

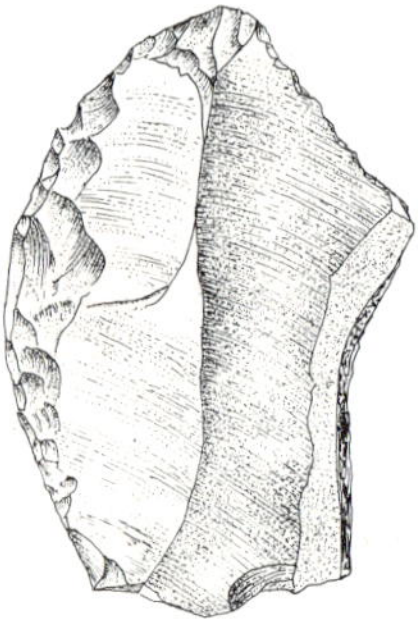

Pointed tool

Scraping tool

Skilled Survivors

The Neanderthals were obviously a very resourceful people. They were able to adapt their hunting techniques to the changing conditions.

The number and variety of tools found from this period suggest that these people were skilled at carving, preparing animal skins and cutting up meat.

One distinguished scholar has identified 63 different

Neanderthal tools are often called 'Mousterian', after the site in France where many of them were found. They were made by carefully chipping away flakes of flint.

types of stone tools, which can be divided up into five separate tool kits.

Religion

There is one other new and special feature about the Neanderthals – they had a form of religion. We do not know how long our remote ancestors had been thinking deeply about the world around them and their place in it, but they had now come up with both ideas and rituals to satisfy some deeply-felt need.

It seems that the Neanderthals worshipped bears, perhaps because they were so feared. In some caves, bears' skulls have been found carefully arranged, probably for a ceremony.

Life After Death

The Neanderthals also thought about death. They believed that there was another world where the spirits of the dead went to live. So they placed offerings of food in their graves, together with tools and weapons, to provide for the future needs of the dead person.

One piece of evidence shows that in one place at least, the body had been covered in flowers by the sorrowing relatives.

Neanderthal graves were usually shallow, but were covered with earth and stones. Ibex horns were arranged carefully round one grave. The knees of the dead were usually bent slightly as if the person was asleep. In some graves several people were buried together.

Early *Homo sapiens sapiens* are also called Cro-Magnon, after the rock shelter in France where their remains were first identified.

The Rise of Modern Man

Homo sapiens sapiens, the branch of the human family to which all today's men and women belong, first appeared on the scene about 40,000 years ago and rapidly (in evolutionary terms anyway) spread across the world.

Where Did Modern Man Come From?
We are not certain where modern man first evolved. Some experts look to the Near East. Even in the Ice Age the climate there was quite warm. Remains have been found in a cave on Mount Carmel in Israel, for example, of individuals who, while clearly Neanderthals, have a more modern look about them. It has been argued that, untroubled by the intense cold and the need to adapt to this in order to survive, the Near Eastern Neanderthals had evolved into modern man.

Others disagree, however. They argue that there was not enough time for such a great change to occur. They point instead to the remains recently found in the Omo Valley in Ethiopia. These seem to be of a people who are a mixture of Upright Man and modern man. So Neanderthals and modern man may have had the same ancestors, but developed separately along rather different lines.

What Happened to the Neanderthals?
As modern man spread across Europe the Neanderthals disappeared. These early modern people, who we call Cro-Magnon, had better tools and weapons and usually travelled in larger groups. Did they actually kill off the Neanderthals? Or did they just take over the best hunting grounds, leaving the Neanderthals to starve? Maybe the Neanderthals were doomed, because they were so suited to life in the Ice Age they could not change when the Ice Age ended. But perhaps they did not all disappear quite without trace. A few may have intermarried with tribes of *Homo sapiens sapiens*. It is possible that we all have the faintest traces of Neanderthal blood in our veins.

Cro-Magnon People

The Cro-Magnons are noted for their tool-making, especially for their blade tools. These were made by striking long, thin flakes of flint from a core of stone. The blades were then carefully chipped away to form the desired tool, such as a knife, or a scraper for cleaning animal hides.

Different styles of blade tools were produced by different groups of Cro-Magnons, some of them at roughly the same time. The discovery of certain styles of tools in a number of different places, shows how these groups moved around.

Cro-Magnons were also the first people to carve tools of antler, bone and ivory.

Travelling Tribes

Like the earlier hunters, Cro-Magnon people worked together, but in larger groups of several families joined as a tribe.

Some tribes specialized in

Part of a tool made from an antler. The craftsman has carved the head of a bison on the side of it with a flint tool, as decoration.

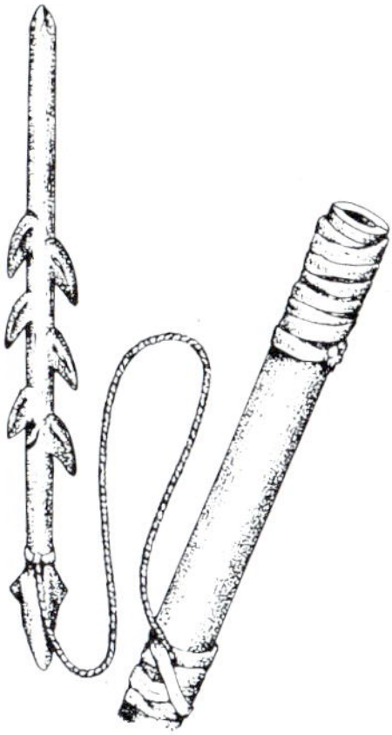

Above: A reindeer harpoon. The barbed head entered the animal's body. The shaft would fall away, becoming tangled in the animal's legs and slowing it down.

Above: A reconstruction of a deer antler headdress found in Yorkshire. It may have been used as a hunter's decoy, or possibly it was worn at tribal ceremonies.

Below: Baited hooks made of bone were used to catch fish. The hook may have been put inside another small fish, as bait.

hunting particular kinds of animals. As the animals moved about on migrations, the tribes were forced to follow them.

A tribe would move camp several times a year, taking all they owned with them. Shells from the Black Sea and the Mediterranean have been found in Central Europe, and certain prized types of flint are found long distances from their places of origin. The tribes may have

travelled specially to get these goods, or they may have been passed on in trade.

Shelters

Cro-Magnons used caves for shelter if they were available. Inside they built tents of skin and poles to keep them warm. In open country they built tents rather like American Indian tepees. The skins covering the wooden frames were held down by stones or bones. In Russia, shelters have been found built of large mammoth bones and covered with skins.

Mammoth bones and flat stones seem to have also been used as work tables. Fires were built from wood, bones and dung, and one tribe had even discovered coal!

Burial of the Dead

The Cro-Magnons buried their dead with care. They sprinkled a red powder over the body, perhaps to make it look more lifelike. The dead person's goods were buried with them. Some people seem to have had many more goods than others. Even the graves of some children were filled with their possessions, which shows they must have had rich and powerful parents. These wealthy people may have been tribal leaders.

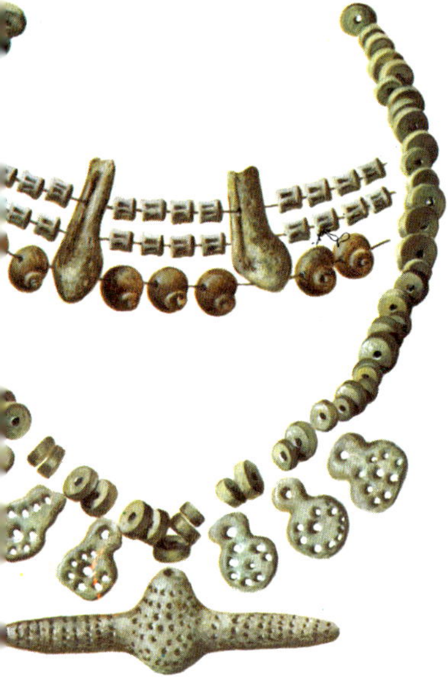

Left: The Cro-Magnons liked jewellery and had it buried with them in their graves. Stones, bones, ivory, shells and teeth were used to make beads and pendants. Carved ivory bracelets have also been found.

The first needles were found on Cro-Magnon sites. The picture below shows the kind of clothes they probably made. They made bone pins to fasten their cloaks. Finds in graves show that garments and caps often had beads sewn all over them as decorations.

Stone Age Artists

Carvings and sculptures found at Cro-Magnon camp sites and in their graves, reveal that some of these people were talented artists.

Antlers, bones and ivory were carved, and a mixture of clay and ground up bones was made into statuettes and then baked hard.

Animal Art

The favourite subjects of these ancient artists were the animals on which their lives depended. They had clearly studied the animals very carefully when hunting them, so their carvings are often very lifelike.

Pictures of animals were used to decorate tools and weapons of all kinds. They were carved as statuettes, as well as in outline and as a raised surface on the walls of caves.

Deep in a cave in France a life-size clay figure of a bear had been made. It was peppered with holes. Perhaps young warriors threw spears at this statue as a part of some hunting ceremony.

Venus Figures

Humans were less popular subjects for carving, but there are more carvings of women than of men. Some are very finely done heads. There are also full length figures. Of these, the most famous are called 'Venuses' after Venus, the Roman goddess of beauty.

This woman's head was delicately carved in mammoth ivory. It is about 24,000 years old.

A bison carved from an antler. You can feel the artist understood and respected the strength of the creature.

The artists who made the Venus figures took great care when carving the naked bodies. These women are portrayed with very generous curves indeed!

Some people think that they represent women who are going to have babies. The carvings may have been a form of magic to ensure that many babies were born to the tribe. Other people say the figures are of a great Mother Goddess. On the other hand, they might just show the type of women the Cro-Magnons considered to be the most beautiful.

Abstract Art

Some objects are carved with dots and abstract patterns. One expert believes that these patterns are a record of the phases of the Moon and of the seasons. He suggests, in fact, that they are records of an early form of calendar. But many other experts refuse to accept this idea.

Painted Caves

The most fascinating examples of art left by the Cro-Magnons are paintings done on cave walls. The artists made most of their paints from different coloured earths mixed with water, but for black they used soot. Twigs, hairs and fur were probably used for brushes.

Some artists simply left prints of their hands dipped in paint. Others outlined their hands. There are a few paintings of human figures,

A cave artist must have had to paint his pictures by the light of many small lamps.

but most are detailed pictures of the animals they hunted.

The strange thing about these paintings is that they were done in the deepest parts of the caves where it is too dark to see them. We can only guess that these paintings had a special purpose.

Art and magic

Some of the animals shown are females who are about to give birth to young. Perhaps magic was meant to ensure that there were plenty of animals to be hunted the following year.

Other animals have spears and arrows in them. These could have been done to gain success in hunting through magic. One picture shows a hunter dressed in a bison skin, close to a herd.

In one cave in France two beautifully modelled clay bison were found. Nearby on the floor were small heel prints, as if children had been dancing. This and similar finds suggests the caves were used for special ceremonies, such as those marking the time when a child becomes an adult.

In one cave there is a picture of a man wearing a deer skin and antlers. He may have been a priest, or a magician.

The Ice Melts

About 10,000 years ago, the Ice Age finally lost its grip on Europe and the climate became warmer and damper. So much ice melted that the level of the sea was raised once more. Many land bridges and other low-lying areas were swamped as the sea swept in. Asia and America became separate continents again, and Britain was cut off from Europe.

The plant life changed and great forests spread over Europe once more.

A Change in the Menu

With the changing climate many animals such as mammoths, elks and cave bears died out. They were replaced by smaller animals like deer, wild cattle and pigs.

Hunters had to learn the different habits of these creatures, which do not live in great herds. Because they were harder to hunt, people also had to find other food.

Small game, such as hares and birds of all kinds, were caught in traps. Even some snails were found good to eat. People living by water ate a lot of fish, while those on the coasts also ate shellfish and hunted seals.

There were now also many kinds of trees, so nuts became an important food.

New Weapons and Tools

To help with their new way of life, people invented new tools and weapons. Remains have been found of bows and arrows, throwing sticks and animal and fish traps. Fish hooks and nets were used and sledges were made for carrying heavy loads. People also had skis so they could move about in bad weather.

Further south, in the warmer climate, other changes in the way of life had begun.

As their way of life changed, people stopped doing cave paintings. The only evidence of art from this time is small painted pebbles.

Man's Best Friend

Around this time people also began to tame some wild animals. Most people agree that the dog was the first animal to become domesticated.

Changes in size and shape took place in tame animals. In the case of the dog, for example, the muzzle became shorter, but this happened very slowly.

A New Way of Life

The process by which man first got the idea of taming and raising animals for meat was probably like this:

One day a hunter killed an animal; let us imagine it was a wild sheep. Then he found she had a baby with her. He did not need any more meat that day, so instead of killing the lamb, he took it home and fed it until it was bigger, then killed it. Slowly the idea dawned that he would have a much more reliable supply of food if he raised animals instead of going out hunting whenever he needed meat.

Sheep and goats were probably the first animals raised for food. As we can see in the picture above, goats are agile animals and can find food almost anywhere, even clambering up into the branches of trees. Soon cattle and pigs were added. Care was taken to breed animals that gave the most meat, milk and wool. Later, ducks and geese and beasts of burden were also domesticated.

When and Where

The most likely area for the first domestication of animals is the Near and Middle East, because this is where the wild ancestors of sheep, goats, cattle and pigs were all to be found. The evidence available at present suggests that this was well under way by 7000 BC.

The effect of having a regular supply of meat, milk, hides and wool would have made life much less uncertain, but people would still have had to move around to find water and pasture for their animals.

Life in South America

The domestication of animals probably happened later in America and appeared first in South America. Llamas were used there as beasts of burden. The two main sources of meat were guinea pigs and turkeys. Dogs were used for hunting and in some places for eating too!

Below: The Fertile Crescent, an area in the Near East where man's first attempts at farming are found.

Herding animals was followed by growing crops and so people eventually became farmers.

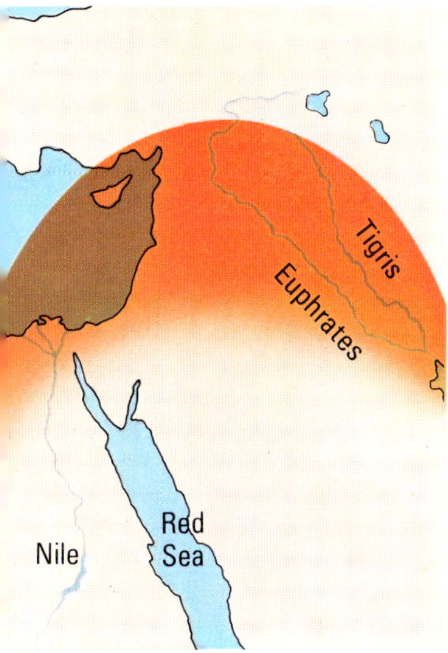

The First Farmers

Gathering plants, seeds and roots for food was the task of the women. There came a time when they must have realized that if the seeds of some plants were sown, the plants would grow again.

If a tribe regularly stayed at a place with plenty of water, some of the women may have deliberately sown seeds to grow crops to gather when they came that way again the next year. Thus, the idea of farming was born.

Grain and Vegetables
The wild ancestors of wheat and barley grew in the Near East. These were the first plants to be grown domestically. Cultivation of plants began at the same time, or just a little after, the domestication of animals.

The first farmers were careful only to sow seeds from plants that had given a high yield. Thus, over the years they produced new, high yield varieties.

Very soon peas, beans and other vegetables were being grown for food. All have high yields and are very good, nourishing foods.

Left: Grain was ground between two stones to make a very coarse type of flour for baking.

In the Far East, rice was grown instead of wheat and barley. In South America maize and potatoes were the plants most widely cultivated.

A whole new range of tools was needed for farming work. Weighted, pointed sticks were used for digging. Hoes were made of wood. Flint blades were set in wooden handles to cut grain stalks and the grain was ground to flour between two stones.

A Farming Revolution

Because farming changed people's whole way of life and spread very rapidly (in historical terms anyway) the introduction of farming is usually referred to as a revolution.

This does not mean that everyone stopped hunting to become farmers overnight. Hunting went on to help fill the larder, and there are still people today who only hunt and gather food.

This chart shows how long it took for farming to spread to different parts of the world.

YEARS BC	EUROPE	NEAR EAST	AMERICAS
3000	First farming, northern Europe		No villages until 1500 BC
4000	First farming, central Europe		
5000		First settlements in Sumer and Egypt; first irrigation	Cultivated maize, Mexico
6000	First farming SE Europe Domesticated cattle, Greece: 6500 BC	Permanent villages; domesticated animals and plants	First cultivated plants, Peru First cultivated plants, Mexico
7000		Seasonal villages	

The First Villages

If you are going to plant crops, you have to stay near them to look after them and make sure no one harvests them before you do. Clearly, if you are going to stay in one place permanently it is worth building yourself a house that is going to last. In the Near East, people learnt to make bricks of mud. In Europe, where there were more trees, people built houses of wood (below). They cut down parts of the forests to make room for fields, and settled in these clearings for about ten years. When the soil became exhausted the people moved to a new site.

Because farming provided a regular food supply, more people survived and there was enough food for large groups to live together in a small area. In this way, the first villages came into being.

Given reasonable luck, a village could produce more food than it actually needed. This meant that it could support

some people who did not work as farmers themselves. Also, because the food supply was more reliable, farmers had more spare time than hunters and gatherers ever had.

Craftsmen and Leaders

If a person was really skilled at some craft other than farming, he or she would work at that. The farmers paid them in food for the goods they made. At one early village, workshops have been found belonging to a butcher, a bone toolmaker, a bead-maker and other craftsmen.

With many people living close together in villages, there were many more opportunities for quarrels to arise. So someone was needed with the power to settle quarrels, make rules, organize the work and lead the villagers if they were attacked. Such men became chiefs. The people paid for their services with a part of the harvest.

These early farmers were also prepared to pay other men and women, who understood the ways of the gods and goddesses, to make sure that the harvests were good.

New Skills from Old

The early hunters knew how to make baskets. Sometimes they lined them with clay to stop things like seeds from dropping out.

Suppose that one day such a basket fell into a fire. When it came out the clay would have survived but would be burnt hard so that even water would not seep out.

Villagers began to experiment with baking clay, and the first pottery was made in about 7000 BC.

Pots for Everything

Pots are heavy and break easily, so they are of no use to hunters who are often on the move. But they are of great value to villagers. You can carry and store water in pots, as well as grain and other foods. Provided you put a stopper in the top, your store is safe from mice and insects.

Pots could also be used for cooking and this led to new ways of preparing food.

Simple pots were made at

People learnt to shape pots by turning the clay on a wheel. The clay was mixed with water and a binder such as chopped straw, which made the clay stronger.

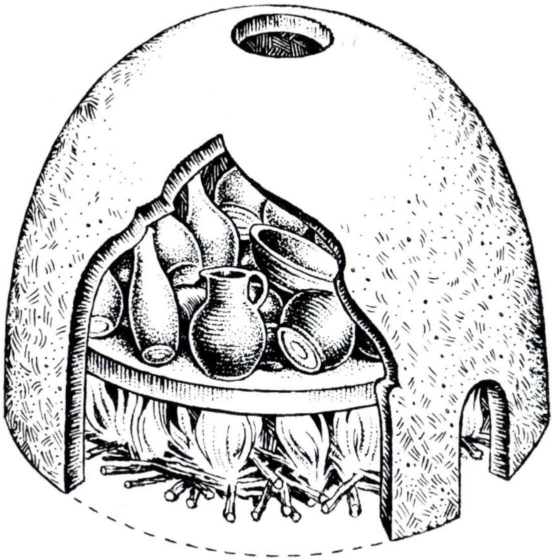

home; then craftsmen began making decorative designs.

Pots were fired in a kiln (above). The first pots were very simple shapes and had little decoration, but soon potters began making highly decorated pots in many shapes and sizes (below).

How a Pot was Made

It probably took many experiments to discover that mixing clay with some other material, such as sand or straw to bind it together made stronger pots.

Early pots were made by rolling the clay into long sausage-like strings and coiling them round to form the pot. The sides were then smoothed and the pot fired.

Much better shapes were obtained when potters began working the clay on a wheel.

Firing was another job that needed skill, or the pots cracked. But people found

out how to build kilns, like the one on page 63, that baked the pots evenly.

Basket-Making

Using strips of hide and plaited grasses, ancient hunters could bind things and knot cords to make nets. Basket-weaving grew from such skills. Baskets are light to carry, so the few goods owned by a hunter's family could be packed in one when they moved camp.

The first villagers also used baskets to carry things, and they learnt to make mats from woven grass. Grain was often stored in mat-lined pits and mats were spread over the floors of their homes.

This model of women at work in a weaving shed comes from ancient Egypt. Egyptian linen was famous for its fine quality.

Spinning and Weaving

People began to weave cloth at about the same time as they started making pottery.

In order to weave, you must first find out how to make the thread. Wool, for example, has to be combed. The fibres are then twisted to form a strong thread. At first this was done with the fingers and wound on to a stick. Then a stick with a weight on the end of it (a spindle) was used to twist or spin the thread.

After the threads have been spun they are woven on a frame, called a loom, on which the threads can be kept stretched out.

The first looms are pictured on pieces of early Egyptian pottery. They were stretched flat on the ground. These are called horizontal looms. Later, upright or vertical looms were invented. These neeeded weights to keep the threads hanging taut.

The production of fine cloth became a highly skilled craft.

Using Materials

Wool may have been the first material used to make cloth, but flax fibres were used to make linen in Egypt at an early date.

The first evidence for cotton does not appear until about 2500 BC, in India, and the discovery of silk came much later than this, further east, in China.

Although cloth was first used for making clothes, people soon found other uses for it, such as bedding, rugs, wall hangings and making sails for ships.

Many people still make baskets today in much the same way as our ancestors made them thousands of years ago.

Towards Today

Man had been using stone tools and weapons for thousands of years. The discovery and use of metals meant an enormous advance in civilization. At first, people just hammered lumps of metal into rough shapes. Then it was discovered that metal could be melted and poured into moulds, where it would harden into any shape that was needed. Also, the use of moulds meant that the same object could be produced quickly and easily, time after time. Man had discovered mass-production!

A copper mine and furnaces in the Austrian Alps in 1200 BC. The metal ore was crushed and washed to separate it from the rock before smelting.

But this new-found skill did not happen all at once. While some societies were producing sophisticated metal tools and weapons for their craftsmen and warriors, other parts of the world remained in the Stone Age.

The Art of Metal-Working

Although people discovered that lumps of metal ore could be beaten into shape and used in much the same way as stone tools, the true art of metal-working did not begin until it was realized that metal could be melted down.

Heating metal to a high enough temperature to melt it is a difficult task. People must have used the knowledge they had gained in building pottery kilns to help them build furnaces for smelting metal.

The earliest metals used were copper and gold, then came silver. Soon it was discovered that a mixture of copper and tin made a harder metal called bronze. Iron did not come into use until many centuries later. Copper was being smelted in some areas in south-eastern Europe as early as 4500 BC, but it took about 3000 years to reach northern Europe.

From Village to Town

While the very first experiments with metal were getting under way, farming and other crafts in the Near East were already well developed.

People had already begun to barter (exchange) their surplus food crops for objects that they were not able to make for themselves, or for materials that could not be found locally. Once such trading had begun it grew rapidly.

Some villages became the centres for trading and people travelled to them from outlying areas. These villages were bound to grow bigger and richer. In fact, they grew into towns.

The Need for Defence

However, such riches brought danger to the new towns. Bands of raiders would attack and steal the goods or even take over the whole town. So as the towns grew richer and larger the inhabitants felt the need to build defences.

At Jericho in Palestine, they built a ditch and high stone walls with towers, while at Çatal Hüyük in Turkey the town had no streets. People climbed up ladders onto flat roofs, then went down more ladders into the houses (above).

Çatal Hüyük was one of the earliest towns and was flourishing in 7000 BC. The people built shrines to a Mother Goddess and decorated them with splendid paintings. The dead were placed on high platforms in the open. Then the bones were buried in the houses.

The Early Europeans

All these new skills of farming, trading, craftsmanship and metal-working did not reach everywhere at the same time, or in the same order. Remember that the same discovery could have been arrived at quite independently in a number of places.

Farming had developed in south-eastern Europe after about 6000 BC, not that long after its arrival in the Near East. But it did not reach northern Europe until 3000 years later, spreading first through central and western Europe and the Mediterranean.

So whilst the people in countries such as Iraq and Palestine were building their towns and cities, most of the people in Europe were farmers who did a little hunting and fishing and a small amount of trading.

Monuments of Stone

But although these people did not build towns at this time or live together in large settlements, they were nevertheless capable of working together on large projects, especially in the cause of religion.

In Malta, for example, they carved spectacular shrines and tombs from the rocks. Some of these are dated to about 4000 BC, centuries before the Egyptians built the pyramids!

Also, in northern and western Europe, farmers built huge burial places that were used by tribes over many years. These generally consisted of a passage and chamber made of great stones, or of wood and turf where stone was not available. These family burial vaults were usually covered with great mounds of earth. We call these structures barrows. To build them the farmers must have had leaders to organize such large projects and good engineers and architects to design them.

Left: Inside a stone burial vault. This barrow was found at West Kennet in Wiltshire. A mound of earth covered the chamber.

Below: Later, around 1500 BC, European farmers used their skills to build estone circles such as Stonehenge, which is also in Wiltshire.

The First Cities

We have seen that in some respects, Europe was not as backward as was once thought. In the Near East, however, developments were happening that were to change people's way of life everywhere.

The Land of Two Rivers

Along the valleys of the rivers Tigris and Euphrates, highly organized settlements had grown up in which the people no longer depended just on farming for their livelihood.

The soil along the river valleys was very rich and crops could be grown easily there. This meant that there was a lot of surplus food to support craftsmen and traders, builders and administrators and also the priests and priestesses who worshipped the gods.

City States

By 4400 BC a way of life had developed with a distinctly recognizable style of art and goods. This development is called the Ubaid culture and it spread throughout most of Mesopotamia.

But although they had a lot in common, the peoples of Mesopotamia did not unite into one land. Instead, certain towns grew into great cities and ruled the land around them. These were the city states, each with its own king and its own temple, which was the home of the god or goddess who 'owned' the city and who was held in the greatest reverence.

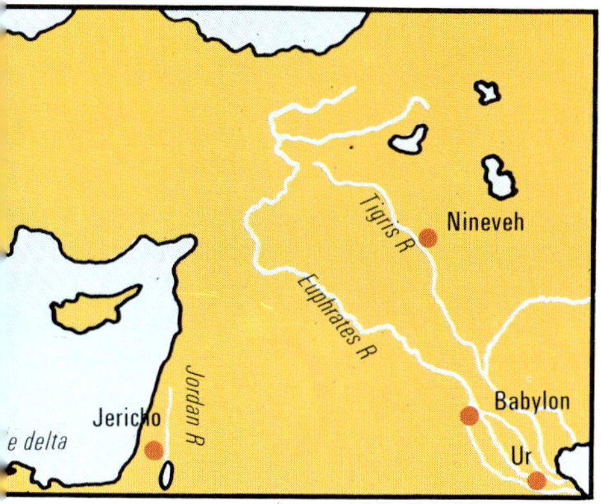

The map on the left shows Mesopotamia, the 'land of the two rivers'.

Mud brick temples later developed into enormous ziggurats (temple towers) also built of mud brick. The one shown below was built at the city of Ur.

On the Banks of the Nile

Alongside the growth of the city states, an even more spectacular development was taking place. The time was coming when rulers would emerge who were strong enough to unite a whole country. This was to happen in the land of Egypt.

The Inundation

Farmers were attracted to the Nile valley where every year without fail the river overflowed. We call this the Inundation. It brought water to a land without any rain. It also left a layer of thick, fertile black mud on the fields. Houses were built of mud bricks, so they were put on high ground to avoid the floods.

As time passed and the number of people increased, farmers sought new ways of producing more food. They managed this by digging out a complicated network of basins and canals. The flood waters of the Inundation could then be stored and used to irrigate a greater number of fields, many of them at a fair distance from the river (right).

Kings of Egypt

A lot of co-operation is needed to plan and build such a complicated system efficiently. Because of this, each settlement along the river valley had its own chief.

The Nile valley is a long narrow stretch of land with desert on either side. As with

the valleys of the Tigris and Euphrates, the incredibly fertile soil alongside the river produced plenty of food both for farmers and craftsmen. The small farming communities gradually grew larger and larger as various chiefs conquered the settlements alongside them.

Eventually, the Nile valley became just two separate areas, Upper Egypt in the south and Lower Egypt in the north, each with its own king.

In about 3118 BC the King of Upper Egypt conquered Lower Egypt and both lands were united. The time of Egypt's rise to greatness had begun.

Further Facts

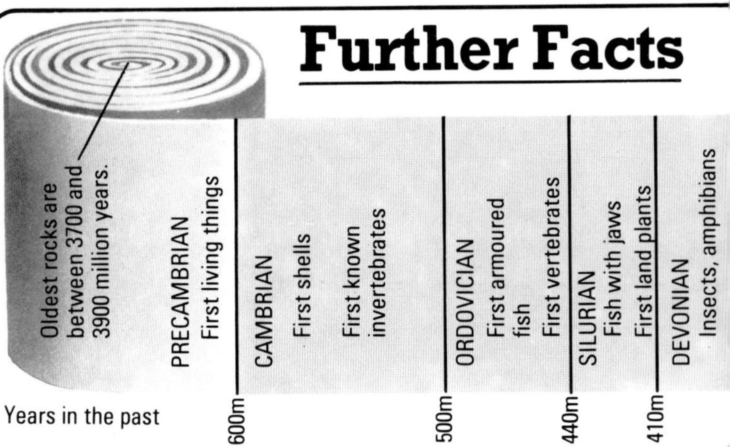

Life on Earth

In the drawing above, the roll of cloth stands for the time the Earth has existed. The rolled up section at the beginning represents the first 4000 million years or so of the world's history, when nothing was alive on the Earth!

The Earth was born some 4700 million years ago. Life only began in the last 600 or 700 million years.

A Watery Start

The first signs of life appeared in the sea, in the form of minute creatures like algae and bacteria.

Later came plants and some soft-bodied creatures like jellyfish and worms.

Rocks Through the Ages

When we talk about early life forms, the time spans involved are so incredibly long that we find it easier to divide time up into periods. These time periods have been named after the different kinds of rocks being formed at the time.

The names of these rock periods with their approximate dates are shown above, together with a guide to the kinds of fossil remains found in those rocks.

You will see how very late even our earliest ancestors arrived on the scene.

Stone Ages

Because the first tools were

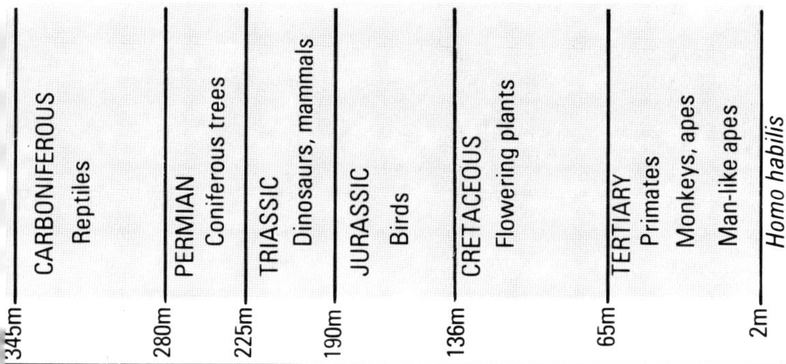

of stone, the early history of the human race has been divided up into periods of time known as the Stone Ages.

The *Lower Paleolithic* or Old Stone Age lasted from the invention of stone tools until the arrival of Neanderthal Man, when the *Middle Paleolithic* or Middle Stone Age began. Then, with modern man, came the *Upper Paleolithic* or New Stone Age. The age of farming that followed is usually known as the *Neolithic*.

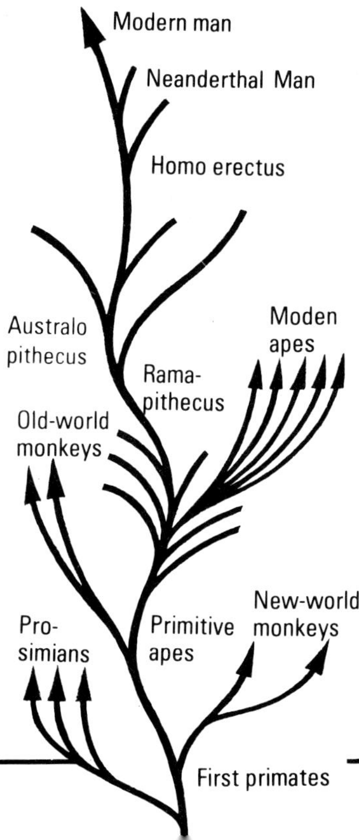

Right: A simplified version of man's family tree. The branches with no arrows belong to the life forms that have died out. The arrowed branches belong to those creatures that are still alive today.

What's in a Name?

All animals are given scientific names. These are often based on the name of the person who discovered them or the place where they were found.

When people are digging for fossil remains of our most remote ancestors, they rarely find a complete skeleton. So they have to guess what the whole creature might have looked like.

If there are no other known examples that are similar to their find they give the creature a name.

Later discoveries may show that two specimens (say a skull from one place and a leg bone from another) that were thought to be two separate creatures are actually the same species. So one of the names must be abandoned.

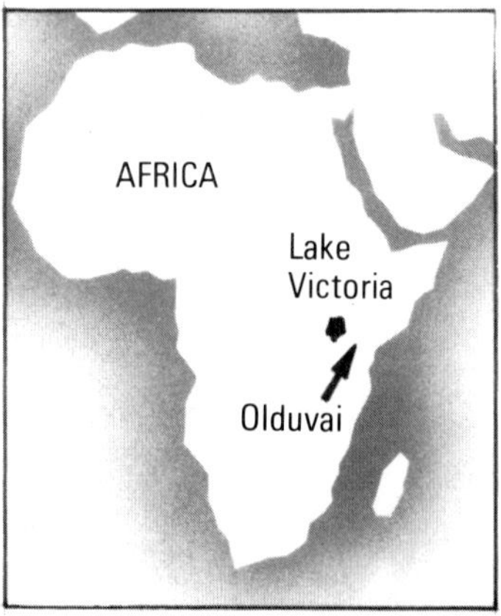

Everybody's Doing It!

It is only natural for excavators to be proud of their finds. They will, therefore, be eager to classify their find as a new species.

Later, others may reclassify the find and put it into another group. This means that the same fossil can often have several different names!

The Leakey Family

Olduvai Gorge is a deep crack in the Earth's crust. This crack is famous for its layer upon layer of rocks that are rich in fossils.

Louis and Mary Leakey have devoted their lives to excavating some of the many fossils in Olduvai Gorge. They have found new kinds of hominids and of men, some of which are much older than people once imagined.

'Dear Boy'

In 1957, the Leakeys found the skull of a creature that they called *Zinjanthropus*

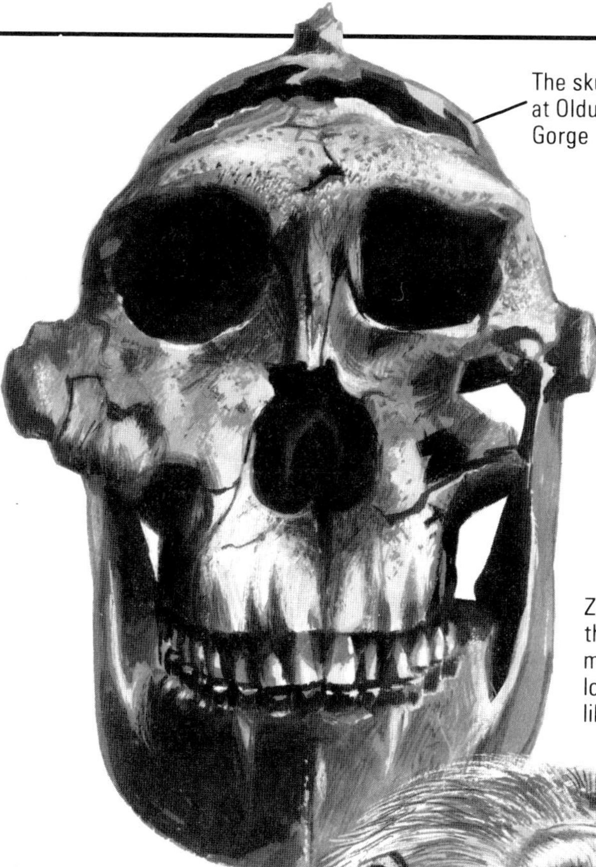

Boisei. Zingi is an old name for East Africa and Boise was someone who gave money to the expedition.

Zinjanthropus is now thought to be another type of *Australopithecus*, but he is also known as Nutcracker Man and Dear Boy!

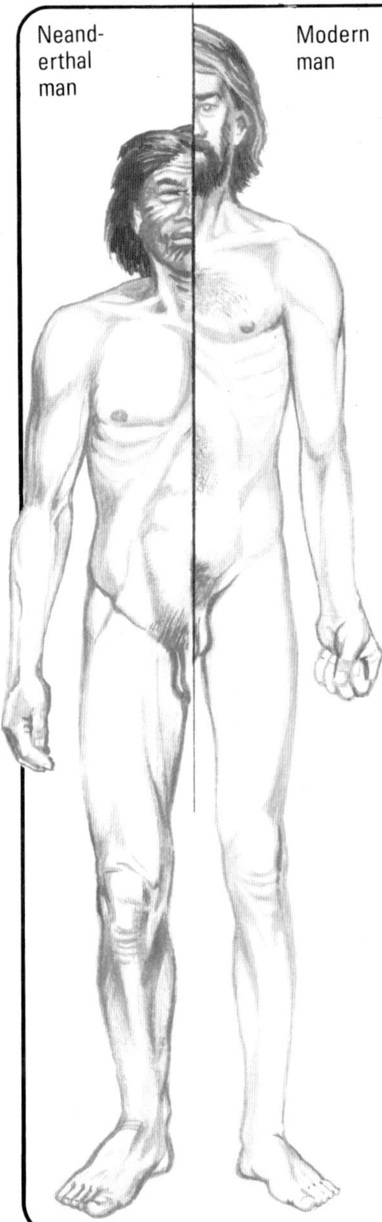

Neanderthal Man and the Swanscombe Miracle

In 1856, in a small quarry in the Neanderthal Valley in Germany, people found the bones of a human creature. Some investigators claimed he was an ancestor of the human race, but many other people were outraged by this suggestion.

The Relative Nobody Wanted

The Victorians, with very decided notions about what was right and proper, simply refused to accept that such a 'savage' could be one of man's relations. Some said he was a violent criminal or an idiot, or someone with a rare bone disease.

Others (unconsciously revealing their prejudices) claimed he was a Dutchman, or a Cossack or a Celt! Today, we have named this creature Neanderthal Man, one of the earliest known forms of mankind.

Neanderthal Man compared in size to modern man.

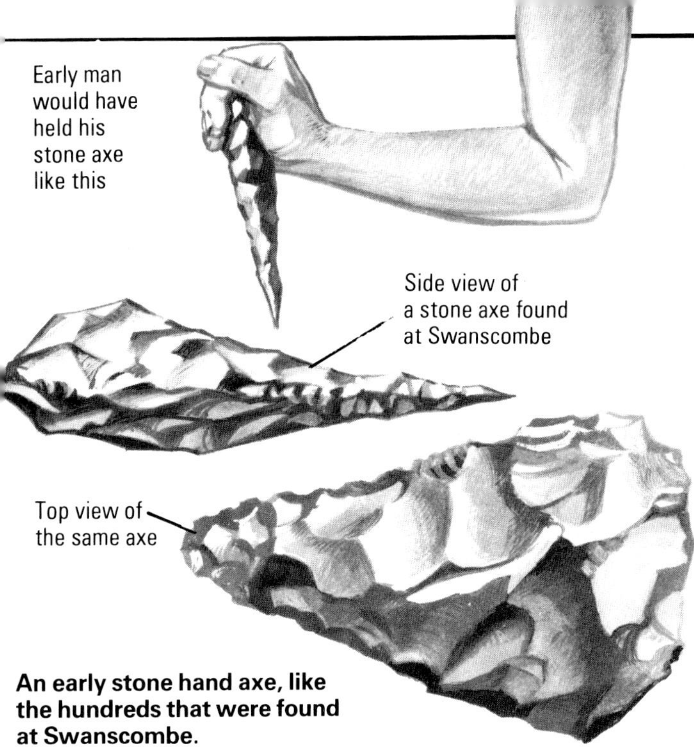

An early stone hand axe, like the hundreds that were found at Swanscombe.

The 'Swanscombe Miracle'
A gravel pit in the Thames Valley has provided some vital fossil clues about the change from Upright Man to modern man.

This site had once drawn animals to drink at the river and early men had come to hunt them there. Hundreds of stone tools have been found over the years, but it was not until 1935 that local cement workers found a piece of skull there.

Nine months later a second piece of skull appeared near the place where the first had been found. It proved to be from the same skull and fitted the first piece exactly.

In World War II much urgently needed gravel was taken from Swanscombe, but something was left behind. In 1955, a third fragment of skull was found and it fitted the other two! Surely a minor miracle.

True or False?

These instruments are used in a laboratory to help identify fossil bones.

Experts in bones have to decide to which group of animals a new find belongs. But they need the help of the scientists in a laboratory to be able to date the specimen and, just occasionally, to help to identify a fake!

Piltdown Man

In the early 1900s experts thought that the first step towards becoming human had been when the brain became larger.

So in 1913, when Charles Dawson, a lawyer and part-time archaeologist, announced that he had found some bones (in a gravel pit at Piltdown) of a creature with a human-size skull but an ape-like jaw, everyone accepted it without question.

Later, as more finds were made elsewhere, it became clear that Piltdown Man was an oddity. His brain was much too big for his jaw.

In 1953, after extensive laboratory tests, Piltdown Man was shown to be a fake. The bones of a modern man and an ape had been chemically treated to make them look ancient. This discovery changed many views on the history of man.

The Taung Baby

In 1924, Professor Raymond Dart received two crates of rocks containing fossils from the Taung quarry in South Africa. In the Bantu language, Taung means 'the place of the lion'.

Professor Dart had been about to go out, but instead he opened one of the crates. There, in the rock, was the skull of a baby animal. It took him over three months to get it out of the rock.

Dart recognized the baby as a pre-human creature. He called it *Australopithecus africanus*, but this new find was largely ignored by other scholars. They had not expected any early changes to have taken place in Africa and they thought the brain was too small for the jaw.

Dart's baby was only fully accepted when the Piltdown fraud was finally exposed.

An artist's reconstruction of the Taung baby and its mother.

The Races of Man

It was only about 40,000 years ago when the physical adaptations that we call racial characteristics began to appear in modern man.

These adaptations arose from the differences in climate. For example, originally all human skin was probably brown, but people living in colder climates did not need so much protection from the Sun's rays, so their skin lost much of its colour.

At one time, these racial characteristics were a way of describing the people that lived in a particular part of the world (see map below). But today, most of the races have become very mixed and spread about the world in different areas.

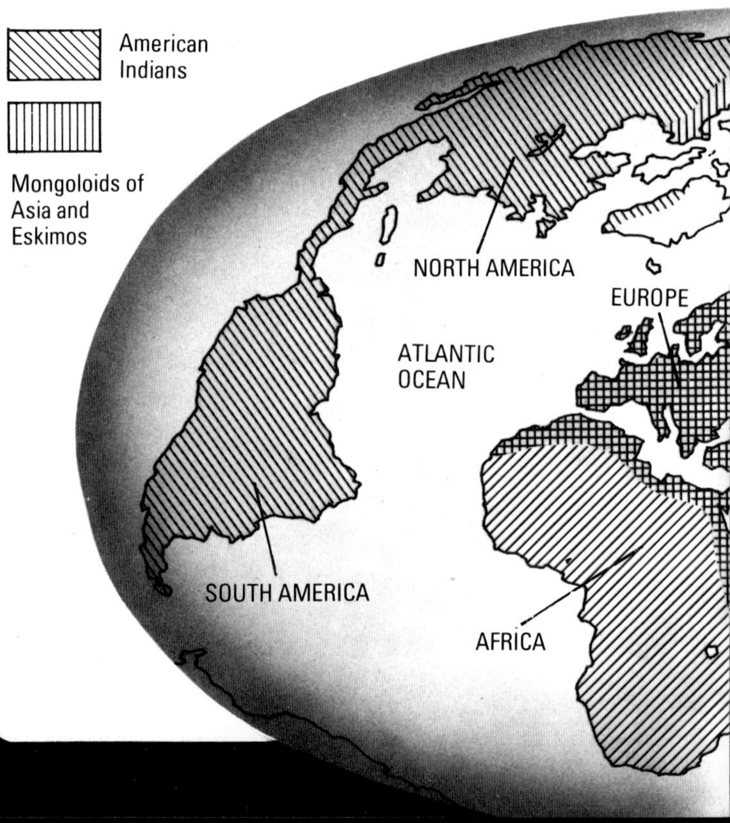

Right: The main racial groups of man: (1) American Indian; (2) Mongoloid; (3) Caucasoid; (4) Negroid; (5) Australoid.

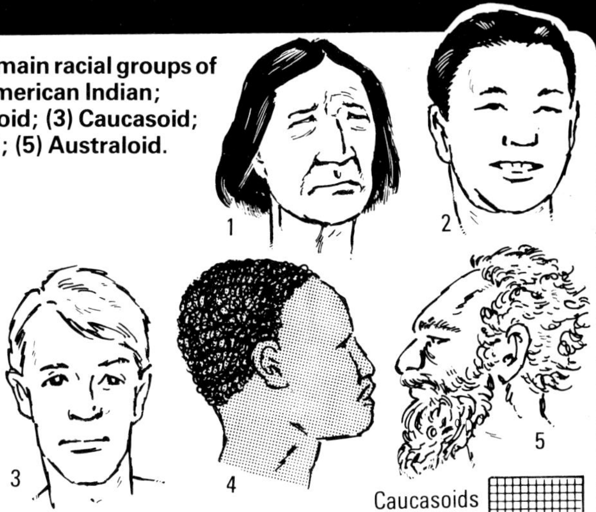

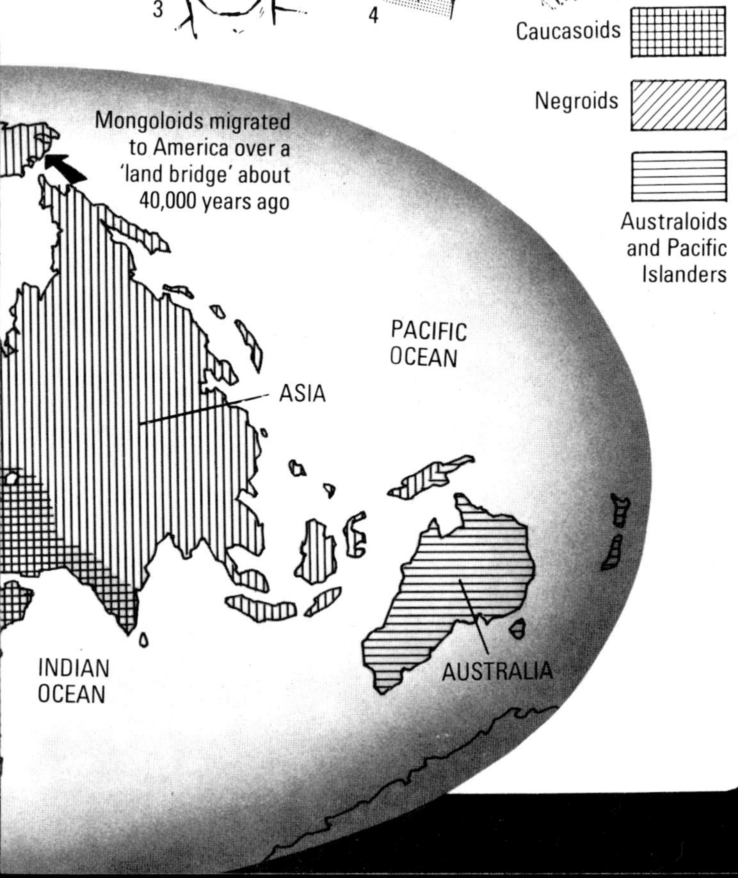

The Powers of Preservation

When most objects fall or are placed in the ground the bacteria and chemicals in the soil destroy them. Only stone, bone and pottery can survive for any length of time. But occasionally something different happens.

Nature's Deep-Freeze
In the frozen wastes of Siberia, the bodies of prehistoric mammoths have been found in near perfect condition. There are even stories of explorers who have dug such mammoths out of their icy graves, and cooked and eaten 12,000-year-old deep-frozen mammoth steaks!

The Tollund Murder
Under certain conditions water will also preserve things, particularly the acid-rich water found in bogs and fens.

In Denmark in 1950, two men were digging up peat when they came across the body of a man. Thinking he had been the victim of a murder they reported their find to the police.

The man had in fact been killed, but the murder (or sacrifice) had taken place nearly 2000 years ago!

'Tollund Man', as he came to be known, was almost

perfectly preserved (left). It was even possible to see the wrinkles on his skin and the stubble of hair around his chin.

Burying the Past

In some cases, man himself has helped to preserve the past. One reason why we know so much about ancient Egypt is because the early Egyptians dug their graves in the hot, dry desert sand.

Well-preserved graves have also been found in colder countries. The tomb shown in the diagram below, was discovered near the Mongolian border.

This and a number of other tombs in the same area proved to be the burial places of a fierce tribe of people. These people had roamed the grasslands of Central Asia in about 900 BC.

Soon after the tomb was built, it had been broken into by grave robbers. The robbers had not bothered to seal up the burial chamber when they left and water flooded down into the tomb and froze.

During the summer the layers of soil above the chamber had kept out the heat and the ice remained.

When the tomb was re-opened in the late 1920s the bodies of two men and a woman were found inside, along with bowls of food, carpets and clothes – all over 2400 years old!

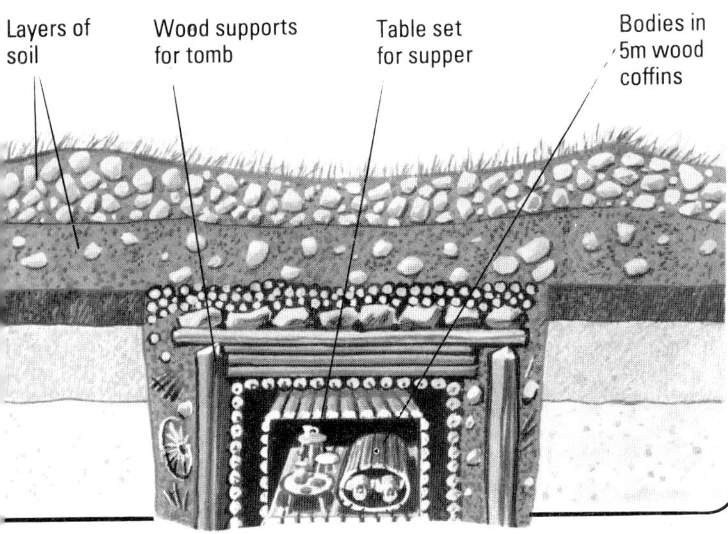

Accidental Discoveries

Most of the beautiful paintings of the Cro-Magnon people have been found in the caves of southern France and northern Spain. But at first, people refused to believe how old they were.

A Painted Ceiling

In 1875 a Spanish nobleman, who was also an amateur archaeologist, was investigating a cave at Altamira. Don Marcelino de Sautuola often took his daughter Maria with him to the cave.

One day, Maria took a candle to a side chamber and glanced up at the roof. Her cry of 'The bulls!' brought her father running to her. The ceiling was covered with several magnificent paintings of animals. De Sautuola guessed the paintings were the work of early men, but it took over 25 years to prove that he was right.

One of the scholars who, in 1901, established the date of the Altamira paintings was a young priest called Abbé Breuil. He dedicated his life to the study of cave art and was the world's greatest authority. Even when he was an old man, Breuil had to crawl uncomfortably along narrow passages to give his opinion on newly discovered cave paintings.

Many of the reproductions of paintings we know well are, in fact, accurate drawings made by Breuil.

Black Magic or White?

About 120 of these caves of art have been discovered so far; more are being found every year. People knew of them as long ago as the Middle Ages, but they believed they were the work of the devil and his demons!

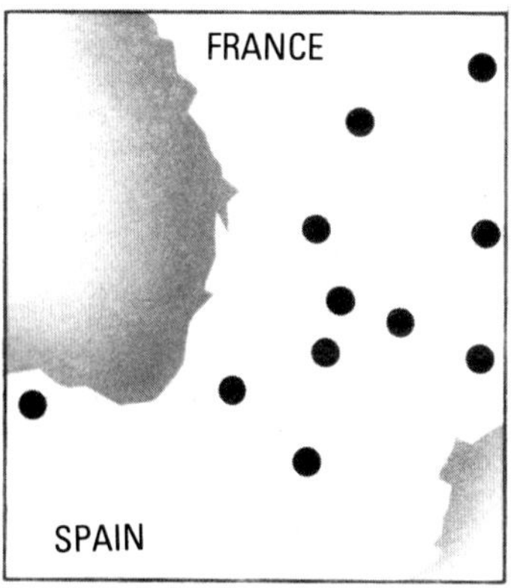

The map shows how thickly clustered are the cave sites in France and northern Spain.

In 1940, four boys were walking along a valley at Lascaux in France when their dog disappeared down a hole. The hole led to a cave, which when it was uncovered was found to contain the most incredible collection of Cro-Magnon paintings yet discovered, with many beautiful and realistic animals.

Patterns, Pictures and Words

As life became more complicated, it was necessary for people to find a way of keeping a record of decisions that were made, of ownership and of taxes.

A Seal of Ownership

To establish who owned what, people began to use seals. They either stamped a piece of soft clay with a flat engraved seal, or rolled a cylinder seal across it. The marked piece of clay was then attached to their belongings, and everyone knew whose it was.

Each person's seal had a pattern or picture on it that everyone would recognize as theirs. This worked well as long as no two seal pictures were alike.

Left and above: The Uruk Vase from Mesopotamia. The carvings around the vase seem to show a religious scene from the time. At the top is a goddess receiving gifts from a priest and a king. Then come more priests and below them the animals, grain and water that supported life.

The Egyptians wrote royal names in an oval frame called a cartouche. This is the cartouche of the great Queen Cleopatra.

Egg symbol indicates that the person was a woman

From Pictures to Words

Objects and numbers can be recorded fairly easily. You can draw an object and numbers can be shown by making a line of small notches. But it is more difficult to record an idea.

This was eventually done by using a picture of an object for the *sound* of its name. The picture slowly came to stand for its sound only and, when linked with other picture sounds, could be used to make a word.

Picture Writing

The first form of writing began in Mesopotamia about 3500 BC. Quite soon, because the pictures were written on clay with sticks, they became just simple wedge-shaped lines. We call this writing *cuneiform*.

In Egypt they used a type of picture writing we call *hieroglyphs*. This style was used throughout the history of ancient Egypt, although they developed two other 'shorthand' scripts as well.

INDEX

Page numbers in *italics* refer to illustrations

Piccolo Explorer Books

Titles include:
Animal Homes
Animal Journeys
The Age of Dinosaurs
The Age of Steam
The Planets
Knights and Castles
The World of Speed
The World of Robots
The Great Ice Age
War and Weapons
Under the Sea
The Midnight World
UFOs
The Violent Earth

Wildlife
The Penguin
The Tiger
The Kangaroo
The Beaver
The Bear
The Wolf
The Hedgehog
The Butterfly

History Makers
Napoleon Bonaparte
Joan of Arc
Genghis Khan
Conquerors of Everest

Guides
Birds
Horses and Ponies
Airliners
Arms and Armour
Shells
Dogs
Racing Cars
Wild Flowers
Trees
Spacecraft
Cats
Insects
Combat Aircraft
Fighting Ships
Military Uniforms
Tanks

Mysteries
Fabulous Beasts
Sea Mysteries
Lost Cities
Missing Treasure
Ghosts
Devils and Demons

Secrets
Secrets of Nature
Secrets of the Sea
Secrets of Space
Secrets of the Human Body